SOLOS FOR THE SANCTUARY
HYMNS

7 PIANO SOLOS FOR THE CHURCH PIANIST

Arranged by Glenda Austin

ISBN 978-1-4584-0022-2

WILLIS MUSIC

EXCLUSIVELY DISTRIBUTED BY

Hal • Leonard®
CORPORATION
7777 W. BLUEMOUND RD. P.O. BOX 13819 MILWAUKEE, WI 53213

Visit Hal Leonard Online at
www.halleonard.com

FOREWORD

These arrangements really began years ago when I was the teenage pianist at a small Baptist church. My older sister and I were "volunteered" by our mother to play the little spinet piano and the Thomas organ. I must admit that together we had a lot of fun coming up with different twists and variations to the hymns and spirituals we grew up with.

Years later, I continue to love and be immersed in all kinds of music—and, I am still playing the piano at church, although I am now fortunate enough to enjoy a concert Steinway. Each week I may play a prelude, offertory, postlude, solo or other special music that is needed. By my estimate, I've played thousands of church services—so I've enjoyed arranging for many occasions. With the *Solos for the Sanctuary* series, I am very happy to share with you some of my favorite piano arrangements that I've compiled over the years and have recently tweaked for publication. Many of them have a little twist of the Southern Baptist/Methodist flavor that I hope you and your audience will enjoy.

Glenda Austin

P.S. My sister is still on the organ. She's also been "upgraded"— and now plays on a Wicks-Quimby 19-rank pipe organ. We still play the occasional duet!

CONTENTS

Amazing Grace

for the William Gillock Association of Japan

Traditional American Melody
From Carrell and Clayton's *Virginia Harmony*
Arranged by Glenda Austin

Reverently, but freely and with much expression (♩ = ca. 92)

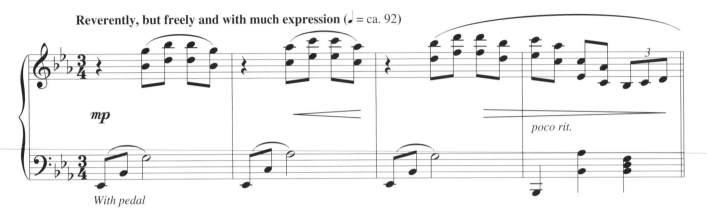

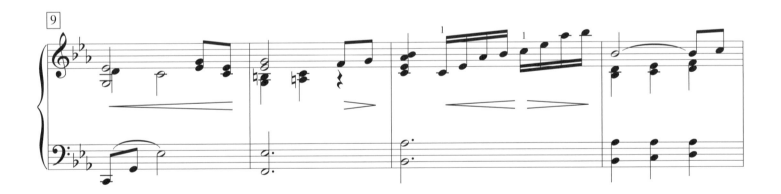

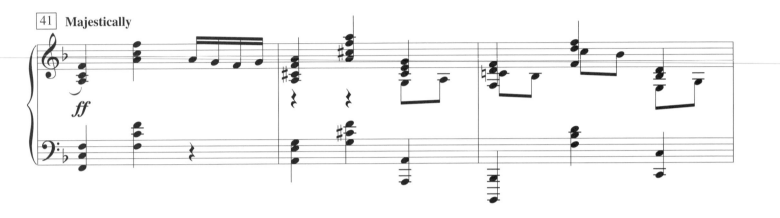

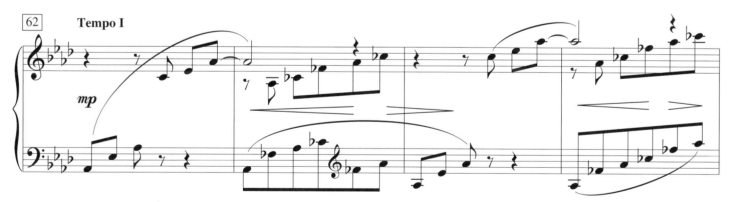

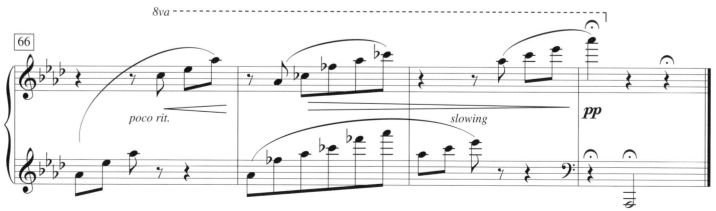

Be Thou My Vision

for Sonya Wilkins

Traditional Irish
Arranged by Glenda Austin

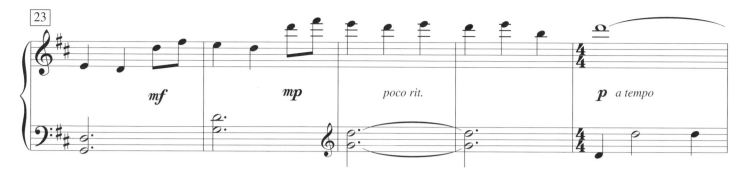

10

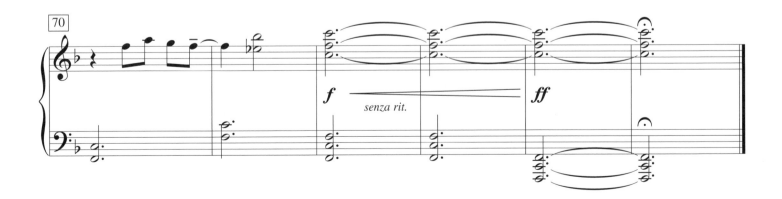

Jesus Loves Me / He Keeps Me Singing

for Melody Stroth

Arranged by Glenda Austin

In a simple style
"Jesus Loves Me" (William B. Bradbury)

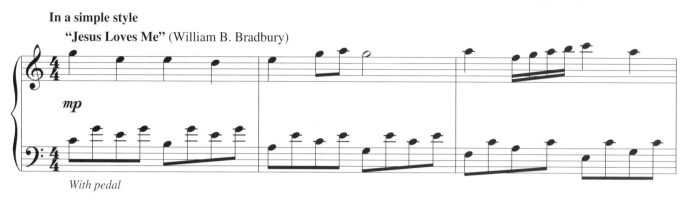

With pedal

"He Keeps Me Singing" (Luther B. Bridgers)

It Is Well with My Soul

for Carolyn C. Setliff

Music by Philip P. Bliss
Arranged by Glenda Austin

With great reverence and expression

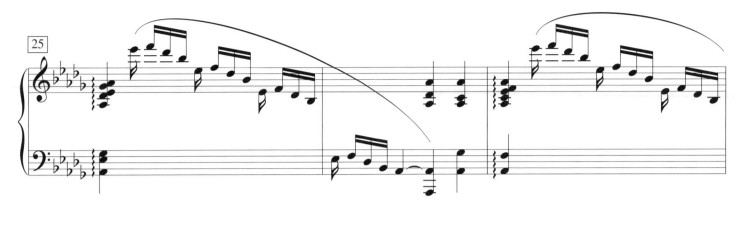

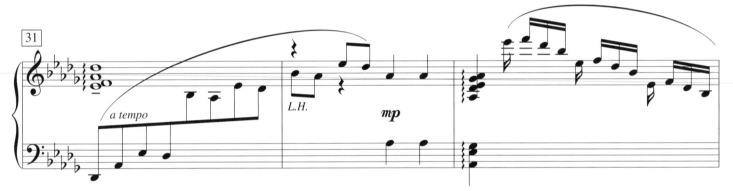

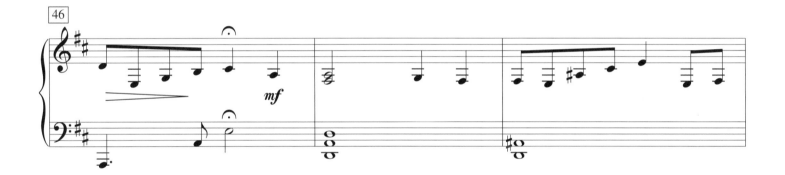

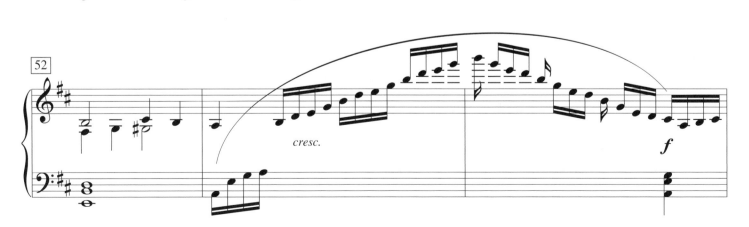

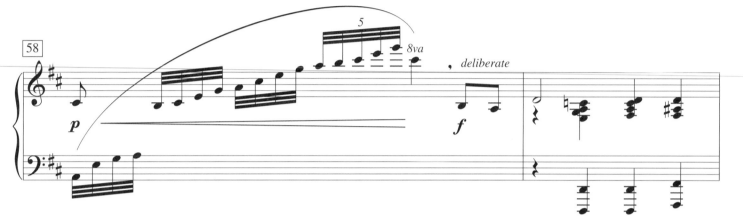

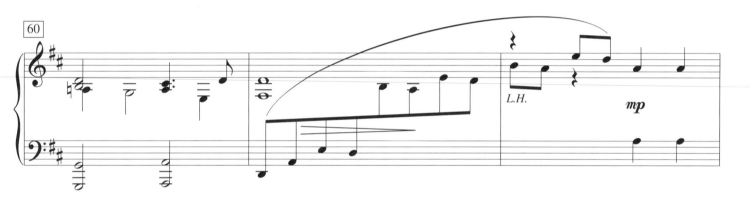

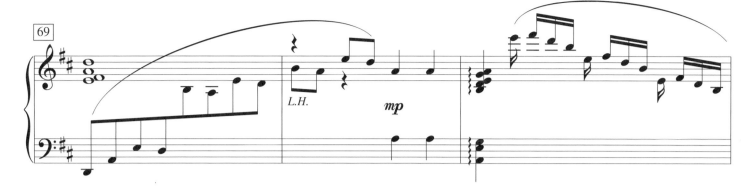

My Jesus, I Love Thee

for Rebecca Murphy

Music by Adoniram J. Gordon
Arranged by Glenda Austin

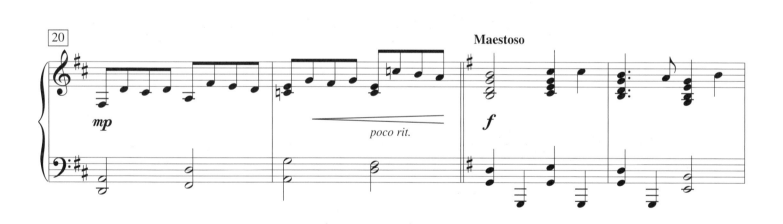

What a Friend We Have in Jesus

for Carolyn Miller

Music by Charles C. Converse
Arranged by Glenda Austin

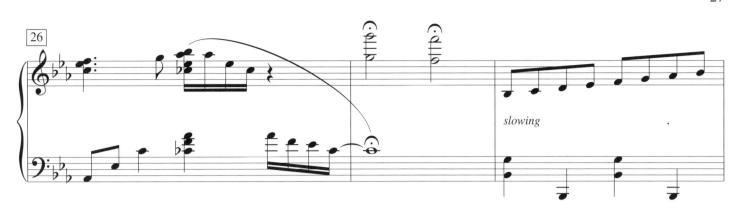

Shall We Gather at the River? /
On Jordan's Stormy Banks

for Debra Snodgrass

Arranged by Glenda Austin

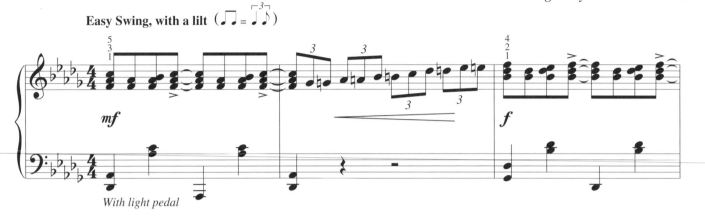

"Shall We Gather at the River?"
(Robert Lowry)

"On Jordan's Stormy Banks"
(Traditional American Melody)

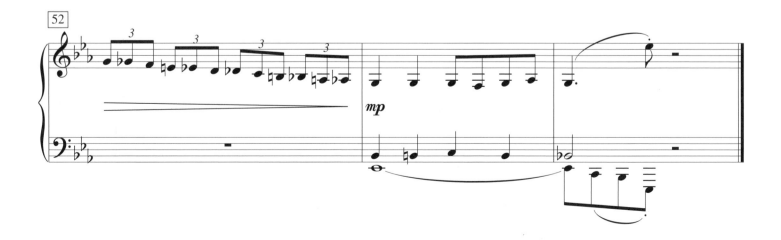